Digital Windows Registry Forensic

By

Dr Issa Ngoie

Introduction

Studying **digital forensics** enables us to delve deep into how the operating system works in order to determine the artifacts left behind by the perpetrator. Undoubtedly, that depth of that understanding will set apart any network, system, or security engineer from their peers.

Digital forensics is a good career for many professionals. According to the Bureau of Labor Statistics, demand for forensic scientists and information security analysts is expected to be very high.
Is digital forensics in demand?

The computer forensics industry is predicted to grow by 17% between 2016-2026, according to the Bureau of Labor Statistics. Due to higher caseloads, state and local government are predicted to hire additional computer forensic science technicians in order to keep up with the demand.

What you need to be a successful digital forensics practitioner?

- Lots of knowledge about computers, technology (contemporary and legacy)
- Professional conduct
- Common-sense
- Ability to think outside the box
- Attention to detail
- Persistence

Maintaining Professional Conduct

- Professional conduct - includes ethics, morals, and standards of behavior
- An investigator must exhibit the highest level of professional behavior at all times
  - Maintain objectivity
  - Maintain credibility by maintaining confidentiality
- Training to update skills – Investigators should also attend trainings to stay current with the latest technical changes in computer hardware and software, networking, and forensic tools

Objectives of computer forensics

Here are the essential objectives of using Computer forensics:

- It helps to :

➢ Recover
➢ Analyse
➢ preserve computer and related materials in such a manner that it helps the investigation agency to present them as evidence in a court of law.

- It helps to postulate the motive behind the crime and identity of the main culprit.
- Designing procedures at a suspected crime scene which helps you to ensure that the digital evidence obtained is not corrupted.
- Data acquisition and duplication: Recovering deleted files and deleted partitions from digital media to extract the evidence and validate them.
- Helps you to identify the evidence quickly, and also allows you to estimate the potential impact of the malicious activity on the victim
- Producing a computer forensic report which offers a complete report on the investigation process.
- Preserving the evidence by following the chain of custody.

Contents

Chapter I; Basics of Digital Forensics

Digital Forensics is defined as the process of :

➤ Preservation,
➤ Identification,
➤ Extraction,
➤ documentation of computer evidence .

which can be used by the court of law. It is also defined as a science of finding evidence from digital media like:

- ➤ a computer
- ➤ mobile phone
- ➤ server
- ➤ network.

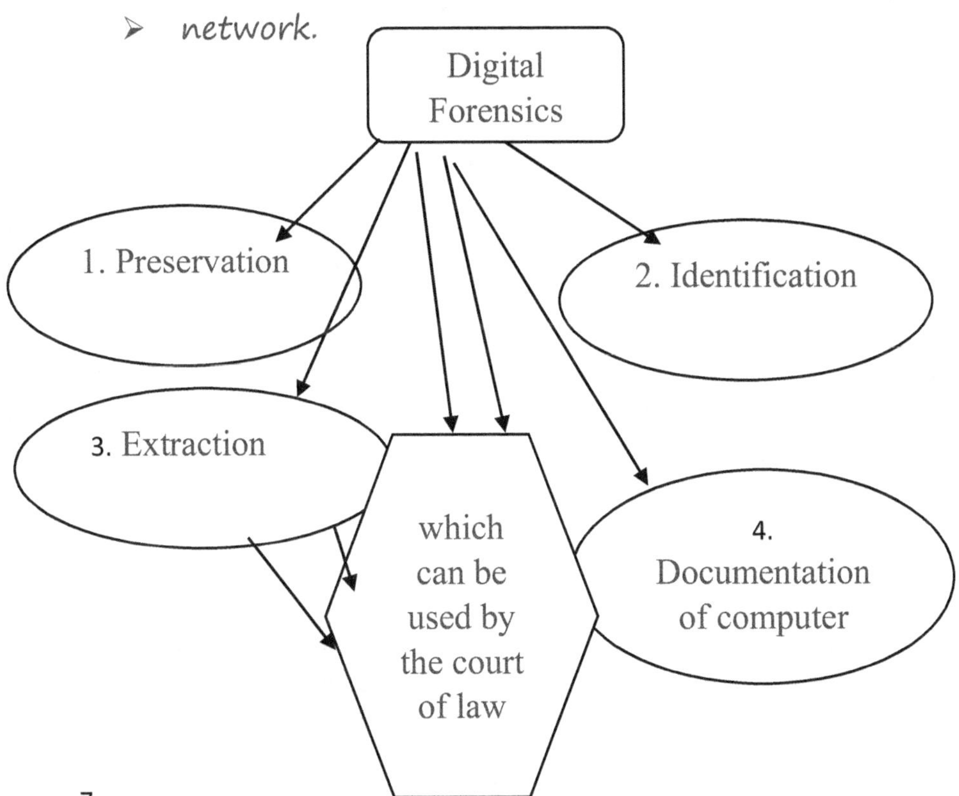

It provides the forensic team with the best techniques and tools to solve complicated digital-related cases.

Digital Forensics helps the forensic team to:

➢ Analyses,
➢ Inspect,
➢ Identifies,
➢ preserve the digital evidence residing on various types of electronic devices.

Developing Digital Forensics Resources ...

- Exchanges information about techniques related to computer investigations and security
- User groups can be helpful
- Build a network of computer forensics experts and other professionals
- And keep in touch through emails / OSNs
- Get professional certifications such as CISSP (Certified Information System Security Professional) (https://www.isc2.org/Certifications/CISSP)

Forensic science, also known as criminalistics

Forensic scientists :

➤ Collect,
➤ Preserve,
➤ analyze scientific evidence during the course of an investigation.

While some forensic scientists travel to the scene of the crime to collect the evidence themselves, others occupy a laboratory role, performing analysis on objects brought to them by other individuals. Still others are involved in analysis of financial, banking, or other numerical data for use in financial crime investigation, and can be employed as consultants from private firms, academia, or as government employees.

In addition to their laboratory role, forensic scientists testify as expert witnesses in both criminal and civil cases and can work for either the prosecution or the defense. While any field could technically be *forensic*, certain sections have developed over time to encompass the majority of forensically related cases.

Forensic science is a combination of two different Latin words:

> ➢ forensis ,
> ➢ science.

The former, forensic, relates to a discussion or examination performed in public. Because trials in the ancient world were typically held in public, it carries a strong judicial connotation. The second is science, which is derived from the Latin word for 'knowledge' and is today closely tied to the scientific method, a systematic way of acquiring knowledge. Taken together forensic science means the use of the scientific methods and processes for crime solving.

"The process of identifying, preserving, analyzing and presenting digital evidence in a manner that is legally acceptable" – McKemmish, 1999

"The use of scientifically derived and proven methods toward the preservation, collection, validation, identification, analysis, interpretation, documentation and presentation of digital evidence derived from digital sources for the purpose of facilitating or furthering the reconstruction of events found to be criminal, or helping to anticipate unauthorized actions shown to be disruptive to planned operations" – DFRWS, 2001

Data vs metadata

Data= can be a set of facts, a collection of images, a string of words, a description of something, etc.,

Metadata= provides meaningful information about data.

Example of metadata: file name, file size,....

Metadata is data about data, Metadata serves many important purposes like data description, data browsing, data transfer, and metadata has an important role in digital resource management. Metadata means machine understandable information to identify, locate and or describe web resources.

Metadata is information stored in almost any type of file. It can include your name, your company or organization's name, the name of your computer, the name of the network server or drive where you saved the file, personalized comments and the names and times of previous document authors, revisions, or versions.

Data can be "raw" or unprocessed and may require hardware, software, or additional documentation to understand and use.

Chapter II: <u>Digital Evidence</u>

> Digital evidence =is information stored or transmitted in binary form that may be relied on in court.

Digital evidence can be found on :

➢ a computer,
➢ hard drive,
➢ a mobile phone,
➢ among other places.

Digital evidence is commonly associated with electronic crime, or e-crime, such as child pornography or credit card fraud.

Digital evidence types

This includes :

➢ email,
➢ text messages,
➢ instant messages,
➢ files and documents extracted from hard drives,
➢ electronic financial transactions, audio files, and video files.

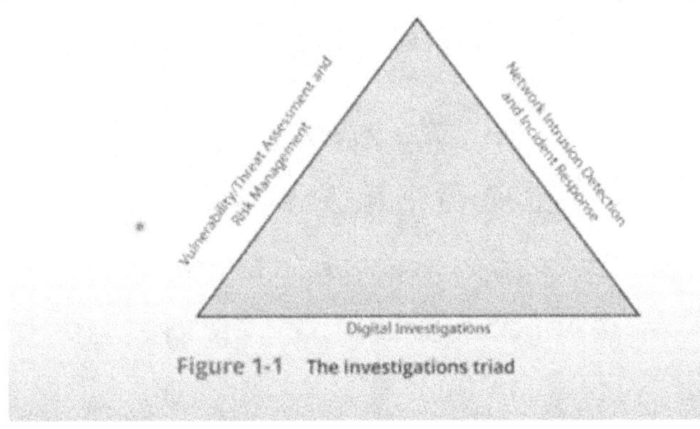

Figure 1-1   The investigations triad

Forensic Process

a. Identification

It is the first step in the exampleforensic process. The identification process mainly includes things like what evidence is present, where it is stored, and lastly, how it is stored (in which format).

Electronic storage media can be :

➢ personal computers,
➢ Mobile phones,
➢ PDAs, etc.

b. Preservation

In this phase, data is isolated, secured, and preserved. It includes preventing people from using the digital device so that digital evidence is not tampered with.

c. Analysis

In this step, investigation agents reconstruct fragments of data and draw conclusions based on evidence found. However, it might take numerous iterations of examination to support a specific crime theory.

d. Documentation

In this process, a record of all the visible data must be created. It helps in recreating the crime scene and reviewing it. It Involves proper documentation of the crime scene along with photographing, sketching, and crime-scene mapping.

e. <u>Presentation</u>

In this last step, the process of summarization and explanation of conclusions is done.

However, it should be written in a layperson's terms using abstracted terminologies. All abstracted terminologies should reference the specific details.

Chapter III: <u>History of Digital forensics</u>

Here, are important landmarks from the history of Digital Forensics:

➢ Hans Gross (1847 –1915): First use of scientific study to head criminal investigations
➢ FBI (1932): Set up a lab to offer forensics services to all field agents and other law authorities across the USA.
➢ In 1978 the first computer crime was recognized in the Florida Computer Crime Act.
➢ Francis Galton (1982 – 1911): Conducted first recorded study of fingerprints
➢ In 1992, the term Computer Forensics was used in academic literature.
➢ 1995 International Organization on Computer Evidence (IOCE) was formed.
➢ In 2000, the First FBI Regional Computer Forensic Laboratory established.
➢ In 2002, Scientific Working Group on Digital Evidence (SWGDE) published the first book about digital forensic called "Best practices for Computer Forensics".
➢ In 2010, Simson Garfinkel identified issues facing digital investigations.

Forensic Investigation

What is a forensic investigation?

Forensics= scientific methods used to solve a crime.

Forensic investigation = gathering and analysis of all crime-related physical evidence in order to come to a conclusion about a suspect.

Investigators will look at :

- ➢ Blood
- ➢ Fluid
- ➢ Fingerprints

➢ Residue
➢ hard drives
➢ computers
➢ other technology to establish how a crime took place.

What Is Digital Investigation? (2)

- An investigation should seek to:
  - Ask relevant questions
  - Resolve lines of inquiry
  - Obtain important answers
- Stakeholders may include:
  - Client
  - Attorney
  - Investigator
  - Regulator
  - Commander
  - Human Resources
  - Executives

Incident Response and Threat Hunting

- Alerted to an incident
  - Data breach
  - Security event

- Can include
  - Unauthorized access
  - Malware/ransomware
  - Application/server compromise
  - Denial-of-Service (DoS)
  - Phishing

- Assume breach
- Known normal
- Built off and into threat intelligence

  - Tools, Tactics, Procedures
  - Endpoint detection
  - Network monitoring
  - Indicators of compromise (IOC)

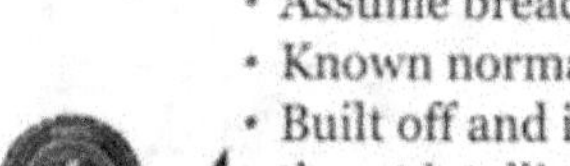

Chapter IV: Types of Forensic Investigation:

❖ Forensic Accounting / Auditing
❖ Computer or Cyber Forensics
❖ Crime Scene Forensics
❖ Forensic Archaeology
❖ Forensic Dentistry
❖ Forensic Entomology
❖ Forensic Graphology
❖ Forensic Pathology
❖ Forensic Psychology
❖ Forensic Science
❖ Forensic Toxicology

<u>Forensic Accounting / Auditing</u>

A forensic accounting investigation aids the victims of fraud or financial crimes. Also known as <u>financial investigation</u>, this kind of analysis uses intelligence-gathering techniques, accounting, business, and communication skills to provide evidence to attorneys involved in criminal and civil investigations.

They investigate by combing through a large amount of relevant figures, searching for irregularities or illegal financial practices. Crimes can vary from tax evasion to theft of company assets.

They also look into insurance claims and high payouts. Forensic accounting services can include:

- ❖ Searching for hidden assets
- ❖ Calculating lost wages
- ❖ Tracing misappropriated funds
- ❖ Performing fraud investigations

<u>Forensic Computer or Cyber Forensics</u>

Computer investigations are similar to <u>electronic discovery</u> (or e-discovery). These forensic investigations recover data from computers and hard drives to solve a crime or find evidence of misconduct. Computer investigators can uncover things like sale of black market goods, fraud, and sex trafficking. Some common situations that call for computer investigation are divorce, wrongful termination, employee internet abuse, unauthorized disclosure of corporate information, and other illegal internet activity. Forensic computer investigations can find information on cell phones and hard drives including emails, browsing history, downloaded files, and even deleted data. One of the first cases in which computer forensics lead to a conviction involved the messages exchanged in an online chat room.

Crime Scene Forensics

<u>Crime scene investigations</u> document and gather any physical evidence found at a crime scene in order to solve a crime or determine whether a crime has taken place. This kind of investigation also includes the analysis of what investigators collect to ensure the evidence is credible and relevant. There are a wide range of crime scene investigators like ballistics experts, who study the trajectory of ammunition and match bullets to potential firearms, and odontologists, who specialize in teeth and bite-marks to identify missing persons or victims of mass disaster.

Forensic Archaeology

Forensic archaeology focuses on human remains that are severely decomposed. They mainly focus on clues they can glean from the bones, including carbon dating to determine their age. From these clues, they can sometimes establish cause-of-death. If a mass grave is discovered or in the event of large casualties, forensic archaeologists can identify the victims using facial reconstruction software.

Forensic Dentistry

Forensic dentists are vital when a victim can't be identified by any other means or when a culprit bites a victim. Since teeth have distinct patterns, the marks left behind can identify a suspect or victim. The shape of the jaw can also indicate age, gender, and DNA can be extrapolated from teeth like with bone marrow and hair. Even if the victim wasn't bitten, physical evidence found at a crime scene may still be useful for forensic dentists. For example, a pencil with bite marks or a half eaten apple might have deep enough impressions to reveal someone's identity.

Forensic Entomology

Forensic entomology is the study of any insects found at a crime scene. Alive or dead, these bugs can reveal where a crime took place, whether the victim had been given drugs, and the time of death. Some insects are only found in specific areas so finding them on a body can suggest whether a body was moved. The presence of larvae in a body can also suggest how long a victim has been dead. If the crime isn't a murder, insects will still occupy untreated wounds in abuse cases or identify the origin of illegally imported goods, like cannabis.

Forensic Graphology

Forensic graphologists study the handwriting on ransom notes, poison pen letters, suicide notes, and blackmail demands. Though age and gender cannot be determined by handwriting alone, it can indicate the writer's state of mind at the time the note was penned. Handwriting can give insights about:

- ❖ Mood
- ❖ Motivation
- ❖ Integrity
- ❖ Intelligence
- ❖ Emotional stability

Slant, size of writing, and the weight of the hand all reflect information about the writer. The phrases and slang the writer uses can also say a lot about location and motive. Forensic graphologists are also used to verify the validity of documents such as insurance claims or police statements.

Forensic Pathology

Ultimately, it is the forensic pathologist's job to find out cause-of-death, especially when it is suspected that the death was not due to natural causes. They perform an autopsy, which involves observing both the outside and inside of the victim. On the outside there may be signs of blows, bruises, bullet entry points, or asphyxia. On the inside, the pathologist will look at things like the organs and stomach contents. By observing these things, a pathologist can determine whether the death was a suicide, murder, or due to natural causes.

<u>Forensic Psychology</u>

Forensic psychology studies the thoughts behind an attacker's actions. Before thinking about how to catch a suspect, forensic psychologists consider why the act was committed. They look at sources of extreme stress in the perpetrator's life that might push them to act violently. They also observe the scene of the crime, which can tell them whether the act was done out of a burst of emotion or was predetermined. Once a suspect is caught, a forensic psychologist can determine whether they are of sound mind. Even in cases of suspected suicide, investigators can examine the life of the victim and conclude whether the act was purposeful or an accident.

<u>Forensic Science</u>

Forensic science is the general term used for all of the scientific processes involved in solving a crime. Some types of forensic science include:

- ❖ DNA coding
- ❖ Toxicology (drugs and the effects)
- ❖ Serology (bodily fluids)
- ❖ Ballistics (everything related to firearms)

A big part of forensic science is the collection, storage, and analysis of fibres, DNA, bodily fluids, and other physical evidence. The roles of forensic scientists have become vital to the sentencing of criminals due to the reliability and accuracy of the evidence they provide. It is also a section of forensics that is constantly growing and changing as technology advances.

Forensic Toxicology

Forensic toxicology studies toxic substances, environmental chemicals, and poison. The drug tests needed for certain job applications are an example of the most basic forensic toxicology. Today, a large part of a forensic toxicologist's job is studying both illegal and legal drugs. Using urine, blood, or hair, they look at the way these substances are absorbed, distributed, and eliminated by the body. They will also look at their effects. For a murder, substances use shows itself in the brain, liver, and spleen.

How data is stored ?

Data is stored as files – the computer equivalent of files stored in a filing cabinet. Files are stored in folders and folders are stored within drives. A storage device is a device that is capable of storing and retaining data even when the computer has been switched off. Here are some examples of storage devices.

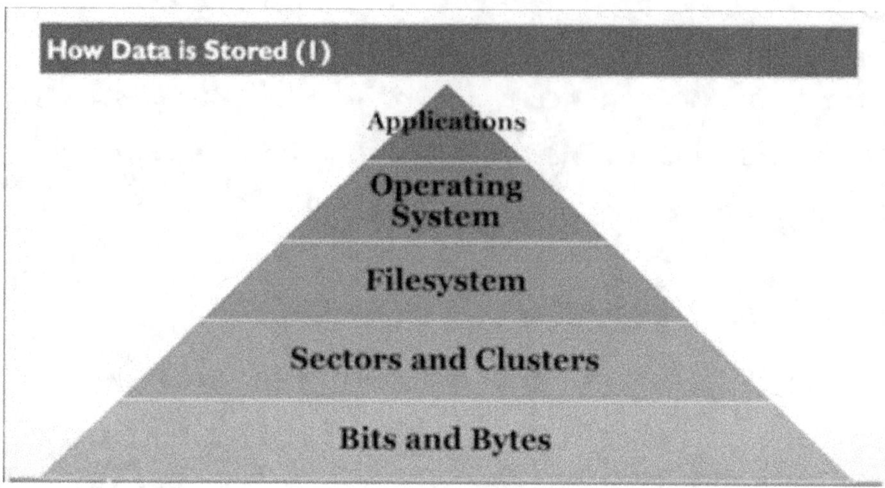

Sectors

- Data on a disk is stored in sectors and clusters
- The number of bytes in a sector is defined in the filesystem header
  - This is set automatically to a default value by the device manufacturer

NTFS
- 512 byte sector

APFS
- 512 byte sector

Clusters

- A cluster is always a multiple of sectors; also defined in the filesystem header
- A cluster is the smallest addressable space on the system

NTFS
- 8 sectors (4096 bytes)

APFS
- 4096-byte block

- Each cluster is labeled by the OS as either allocated or unallocated:
  - **Allocated**: cluster is currently allocated to a file
  - **Unallocated**: cluster is NOT currently allocated to a file

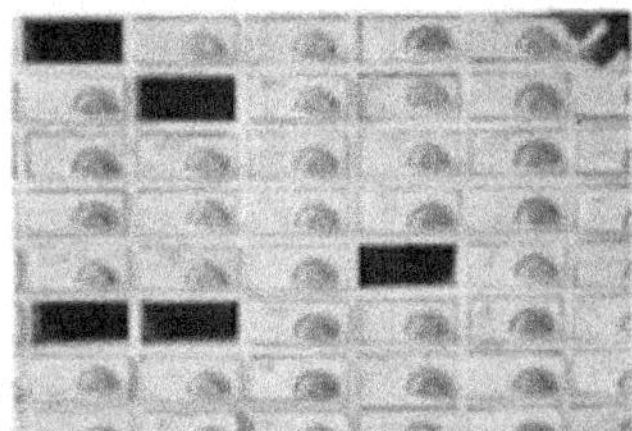

- An unallocated cluster does NOT indicate it has never been previously allocated to any files

- Since a cluster is the smallest addressable space, a new file is created in one or more clusters

- If the entirety of this space is not occupied by the file, remaining space cannot be used by another file

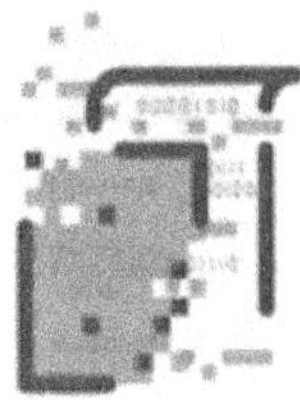

- This remaining space is called "slack space"

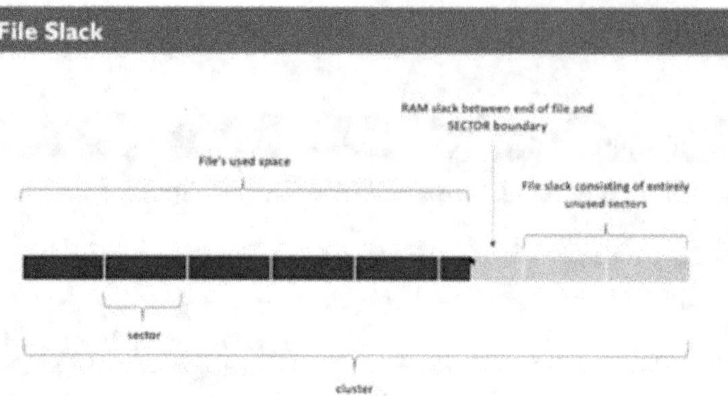

Types of Slack Space

- There are three different types of slack space:

  - **RAM slack** – unused space between the end of the logical file and the end of that sector

  - **File slack** – unused sectors within the last cluster the file occupies

  - **Volume slack** – unused space between the end of the filesystem and the end of the partition that it occupies

What happened when a file is deleted ?

When you delete a file from a standard desktop computer, the file first gets moved to the "recycle bin" or the "trash," which means only that you've placed the intact data in a new directory. You erase the file when you empty your recycle bin. But even then, much of the information remains on the hard disk.

Although you can no longer see the file on the location it once was and your operating system no longer has it, a copy of it still exists in your hard drive. The file will remain there until another file replaces that file in the exact location.

by using special tools, they can find data that hasn't been overwritten yet. However, by using encryption methods, you can ensure your data is kept private, even after deletion.

File systems

Windows

- New Technology File System (NTFS)
- Extended File Allocation Table (exFAT)
- File Allocation Table (FAT32)

macOS

- Hierarchical File System Plus (HFS+)
- Apple File System (APFS)

Where to Find Digital Evidence (non-exhaustive list)

- Desktop computers and laptops
- Servers
- Virtual machines
- Tablets and mobile devices
- Removable media
- RAM
- Network devices and data
- IoT devices, drones, vehicles
- The Cloud

 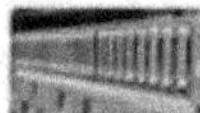    

Typically 8 steps in the roadmap:

1. Search authority (search warrant or an authorisation letter (in case of corporate investigations))
2. Chain of custody
3. Imaging / hashing function
4. Validated tools
5. Analysis
6. Repeatability (Quality Assurance)
7. Reporting
8. Possible expert presentation

Chapter V: _Need of a forensic investigator_

There are a few situations for which hiring a private investigator would be wise:

If you have been accused of a crime: The most efficient way to clear your name is to allow a professional, unbiased source gather evidence.

If you have been the victim of a crime: Evidence found by an investigator is reliable and will stand up in court.

If your spouse is cheating on you: An _infidelity investigator_ can prove your spouse's actions via email, voicemails, and other surveillance, in order to get you the compensation you need.

If you are a business owner: Companies and employers often use _corporate investigations_ because they can uncover sexual harassment issues, lawsuits from disgruntled employees, internet abuse, stolen customer information, or intellectual property issues.

While it is true that almost all police forces have a forensic team on staff, these investigators often handle multiple cases at once. Not only will hiring your own investigator ensure that your case is at the forefront, but they can continue their investigation for as long as you need.

Document and Media Exploitation (DOMEX)

- Acquire, translate, and analyze analog or digital data to generate critical information in a timely manner

- Intelligence purposes

- Time pressure

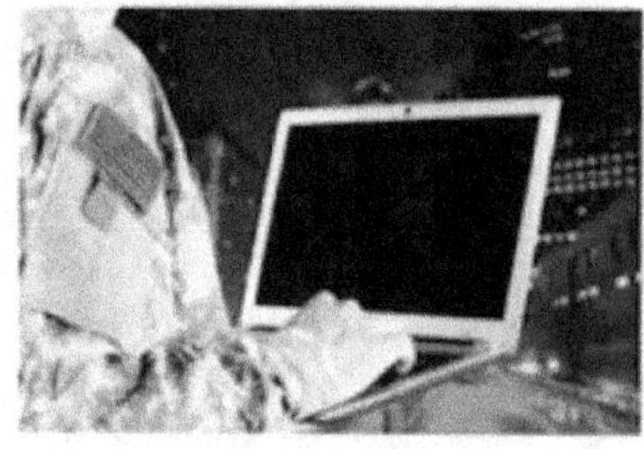

- **Private or corporate investigations**
  - Involve private companies and lawyers who address company policy violations and litigation disputes

- **Corporate computer crimes can involve:**
  - E-mail harassment
  - Falsification of data
  - Gender and age discrimination
  - Embezzlement
  - Sabotage
  - Industrial espionage

- **Establishing company policies**
- One way to avoid litigation is to publish and maintain policies that employees find easy to read and follow
- Published company policies provide a line of authority
  - For a business to conduct internal investigations
- Well-defined policies
  - Give computer investigators and forensic examiners the authority to conduct an investigation

For example, business can avoid litigation by displaying a **warning banner** on computer screens

* Informs end users that the organization reserves the right to inspect computer systems and network traffic at will

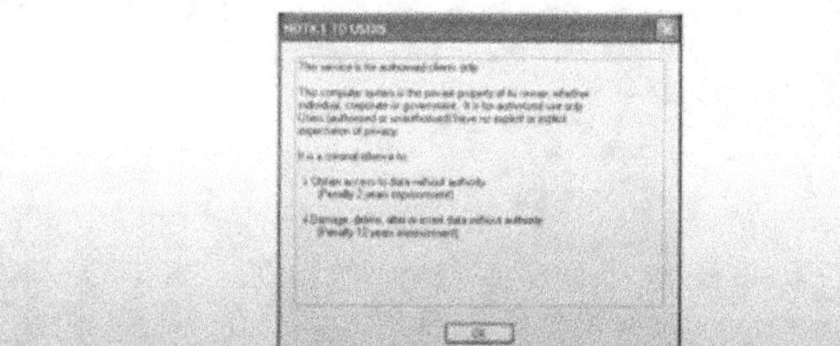

Conducting security investigations

* Types of situations

    * Abuse or misuse of corporate assets

    * E-mail abuse

    * Internet abuse

* Be sure to distinguish between a company's abuse problems and potential criminal problems

* What happens when a civilian or corporate investigative agent

Distinguishing personal and company property

* Many company policies distinguish between personal and company computer property

* One area that's difficult to distinguish involves BYODs: mobile phones, tablets and personal notebook computers

* The safe policy is to not allow any personally owned devices to be connected to company-owned resources

    * Limiting the possibility of commingling personal and company

Chapter VI: <u>Forensic Evidence</u>

What is forensic evidence?

- ❖ Genetic material (blood, hair, skin)
- ❖ Trace chemicals
- ❖ Dental history
- ❖ Fingerprints
- ❖ Witness testimonies
- ❖ Bullets or other potential weapons (ballistics)
- ❖ Shoe and tire marks
- ❖ Illicit substances
- ❖ Documents, files, and records (hospital records, tax forms, job history, etc.)
- ❖ Computers and phones
- ❖ Videos or photographs

- Financial and information system audits to provide assurance
- Audit evidence
- Show compliance to established standards

- A formal inquiry into a specific company, or class of companies by a regulatory body
- A regulator is generally a government entity empowered by law
- Protecting customers and community standards

- Types of investigations include:
  - Inappropriate conduct
  - Misuse of company resources
  - Data theft

- Generally non-criminal

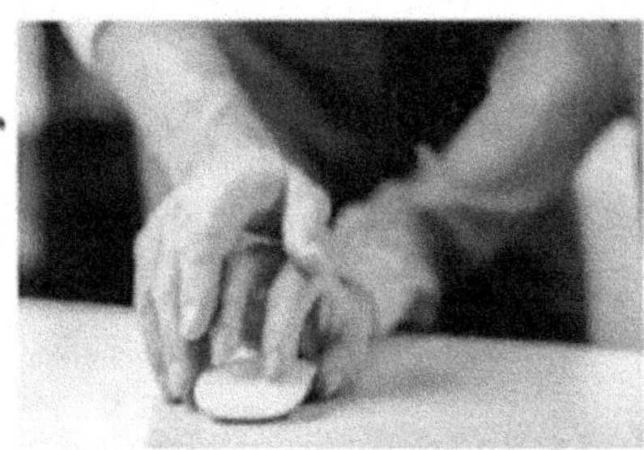

- "Criminal law deals with behavior that is or can be construed as an *offense against the public, society, or the state*—even if the immediate victim is an individual."

- "Civil law deals with behavior that constitutes an *injury to an individual or other private party*, such as a corporation."

- *Any* offense can involve digital devices
  - Homicide
  - Drug enforcement
  - Child abuse investigations

- Analyze data for presentation in court

- Criminal litigation - beyond reasonable doubt
- Civil litigation – balance of probabilities
  - Privileged data and other constraints

37

<u>Challenges in digital forensics</u>

- Rapidly changing technology
- System & application updates
- Device & data volumes
- Recruitment & retention of practitioners
- Mental health
- Ongoing education
- Over-reliance on tools
- Unsupported devices
- Encryption
- Anti-forensics

- ❖ Easy availability of hacking tools
- ❖ Lack of physical evidence makes prosecution difficult.
- ❖ The large amount of storage space into Terabytes that makes this investigation job difficult.
- ❖ Any technological changes require an upgrade or changes to solutions.

<u>Example Uses of Digital Forensics</u>

In recent time, commercial organizations have used digital forensics in following a type of cases:

- ❖ Intellectual Property theft
- ❖ Industrial espionage
- ❖ Employment disputes
- ❖ Fraud investigations

❖ Inappropriate use of the Internet and email in the workplace

❖ Forgeries related matters

❖ Bankruptcy investigations

❖ Issues concern with the regulatory compliance

❖ **Advantages of Digital forensics**
Here, are pros/benefits of Digital forensics

❖ To ensure the integrity of the computer system.

❖ To produce evidence in the court, which can lead to the punishment of the culprit.

❖ It helps the companies to capture important information if their computer systems or networks are compromised.

❖ Efficiently tracks down cybercriminals from anywhere in the world.

❖ Helps to protect the organization's money and valuable time.

❖ Allows to extract, process, and interpret the factual evidence, so it proves the cybercriminal action's in the court.

<u>Disadvantages of Digital Forensics</u>

Here, are major cos/ drawbacks of using Digital Forensic

- Digital evidence accepted into court. However, it is must be proved that there is no tampering

- Producing electronic records and storing them is an extremely costly affair

❖ Legal practitioners must have extensive computer knowledge
❖ Need to produce authentic and convincing evidence
❖ If the tool used for digital forensic is not according to specified standards, then in the court of law, the evidence can be disapproved by justice.
❖ Lack of technical knowledge by the investigating officer might not offer the desired result
❖ Malware Forensics, Email Forensics, Memory Forensics, etc.
❖ Digital forensic Science can be used for cases like 1) Intellectual Property theft, 2) Industrial espionage 3) Employment disputes, 4) Fraud investigations.

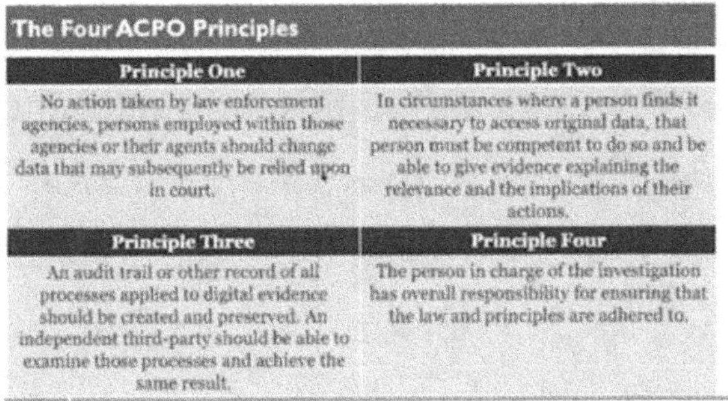

The Four ACPO Principles	
Principle One	**Principle Two**
No action taken by law enforcement agencies, persons employed within those agencies or their agents should change data that may subsequently be relied upon in court.	In circumstances where a person finds it necessary to access original data, that person must be competent to do so and be able to give evidence explaining the relevance and the implications of their actions.
Principle Three	**Principle Four**
An audit trail or other record of all processes applied to digital evidence should be created and preserved. An independent third-party should be able to examine those processes and achieve the same result.	The person in charge of the investigation has overall responsibility for ensuring that the law and principles are adhered to.

Chapter VII: <u>Basic of windows registry</u>

As you are going through your investigation, you will need to know basic information about the forensic image you are searching. To find out more about the image you are analyzing, you will need to look through the Windows Registry.

The Windows Registry is basically a database that stores thousands of records with information, such as the operating system, time zone, user settings, user accounts, external storage devices, and some program data. When you look through the Windows Registry in the next section with REGEDIT, it may appear as though the registry is one large storage location. However, there are several files where the information is being stored throughout the computer.

REGEDIT simply takes these files and records stored in different locations and displays them for you. There are many records in the Windows Registry that will have no forensic value to you as an examiner, but there are some pieces of information that you will find useful. This chapter will walk you through the basic structure of the registry and where you need to look to find information that is valuable to your investigation.

REGEDIT In this section, you will start with the Windows registry utility known as REGEDIT.exe. You can open this by pressing the Windows key+R and then typing in "REGEDIT".

You can also click on the Start menu and type "REGEDIT" in the Search box.

 Note: REGEDIT.exe displays your computer's registry. You should not make any adjustments to your registry unless you know what the change will do to your computer.

 When conducting a forensic examination of a target hard drive, you will not see the same subtrees displayed in REGEDIT. However, most information you come across on the Internet will be notated in a format that assumes you are using REGEDIT.

For example, you may find information showing you the location for a user's home page setting for Internet Explorer written as:

HKEY_LOCAL_MACHINE\SYSTEM\[CurrentControlSet]\Control\TimeZoneInformation

However, if you received information from another examiner, he may have written it as: SYSTEM Hive: [CurrentControlSet]\Control\TimeZoneInformation

Both of these locations are exactly the same; it just depends on how you are viewing them. It is a good idea to start using proper terminology so there is no confusion when you are documenting your findings. The first terms you need to become familiar with are subtree, key, subkey, hive, and value.

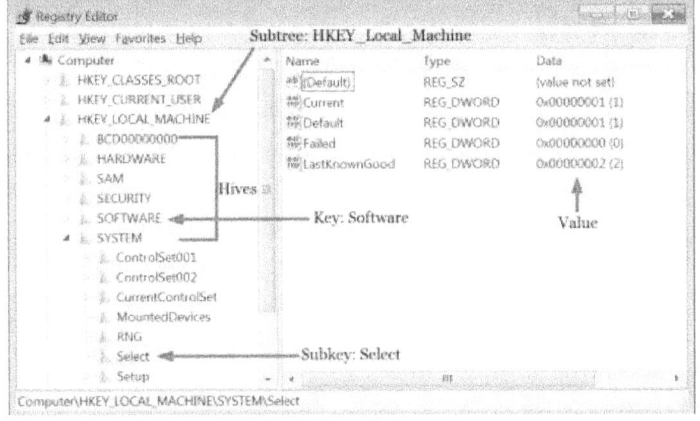

Subtrees, Keys, and Subkeys

There are 5 *subtrees* that make up the Windows registry. The following list contains each subtree, the standard abbreviation, and the type of information found within each subtree:

Subtree	Abbreviation	Description
HKEY_CLASSES_ROOT	HKCR	Contains information about file extension associations and the Object Linking and Embedding (OLE) database.
HKEY_CURRENT_USER	HKCU	Contains user information, preferences, and settings for the user that is currently logged on (in this case, you will see your settings).
HKEY_LOCAL_MACHINE	HKLM	Contains computer-specific information, such as software, hardware, and security.
HKEY_USERS	HKU	Contains user information from the user currently logged in, the default profile, and system accounts.
HKEY_CURRENT_CONFIG	HKCC	Created during the boot process and contains information associated with the hardware configuration.

Below the HKEY_LOCAL_MACHINE *subtree*, there are five *keys*, which are also called *hives*. Below each *key*, such as SYSTEM, there are *subkeys*, such as Select.

Hives

The Windows registry has several system files called hives, with each hive being mapped to a single file. The HKEY_LOCAL_MACHINE (HKLM) subtree contains settings that apply to the local computer's configuration and affect each user that logs on. There are four main hives that are associated with HKLM, and the list below displays the name of each hive and the actual filename associated with that hive:

Hives	Location of Hives
HKEY_LOCAL_MACHINE\SYSTEM	C:\Windows\system32\config\SYSTEM
HKEY_LOCAL_MACHINE\SOFTWARE	C:\Windows\system32\config\SOFTWARE
HKEY_LOCAL_MACHINE\SECURITY	C:\Windows\system32\config\SECURITY
HKEY_LOCAL_MACHINE\SAM	C:\Windows\system32\config\SAM

Note: Backups of the hives are located in C:\Windows\system32\config\regback. Look at the Modified dates of those files to determine if they may contain old information that could be useful to your investigation.

With REGEDIT, you will see a key called HARDWARE. However, there is not a system file that matches this key. The key is volatile in memory, so you will not be able to see it during your analysis. It contains information about the hardware devices that were detected during the boot process.

Values

You need to be familiar with the terms *value name*, *value data*, and *value type*. Each subkey in the registry contains at least one or more values. In Figure 4-1, there is a *value name* of LastKnownGood and its *value data* is 2. The registry also contains different types of data, which is referred to as a *value type*. Here is a list of values types:

Value Type	Description
REG_NONE	No defined value type.
REG_SZ	Null-terminated string that will be either ANSI or Unicode.
REG_EXPAND_SZ	Null-terminated string that contains references to environment variables.
REG_BINARY	This is binary data and it's displayed in hexadecimal notation.
REG_DWORD	A 32-bit number. The values stored are sometimes used as Boolean flags (00 = disabled; 01 = enabled).
REG_DWORD_BIG_ENDIAN	This is a double-word value stored as big endian (most significant byte first).
REG_MULTI_SZ	Array of null-terminated strings, terminated by two null characters.
REG_QWORD	A 64-bit number.

As you look at values stored in the registry, remember that an application can store data in different ways and the interpretation is up to the program. Never assume a value means something unless you have confirmed the setting. For example, you may see a value of 0 and assume that means disabled; however, the programmer might have used the value of 0 to mean not disabled (therefore it is enabled).

User Profiles

On Windows 7 and 8 computers, the user profile is stored in a separate folder for each user under C:\Users\[username]. Each user profile folder contains a profile hive, which is a system file called NTUSER.DAT.

When a user is logged in, the user's NTUSER.DAT file is mapped to the following two subtrees:

HKEY_CURRENT_USER

HKEY_USERS

Under the HKEY_USERS subtree, there are some additional profile hives, which are listed below:

HKU\S-1-5-18	Local System (same as .DEFAULT)
HKU\S-1-5-19	LocalService NTUSER.DAT
HKU\S-1-5-20	NetworkService NTUSER.DAT

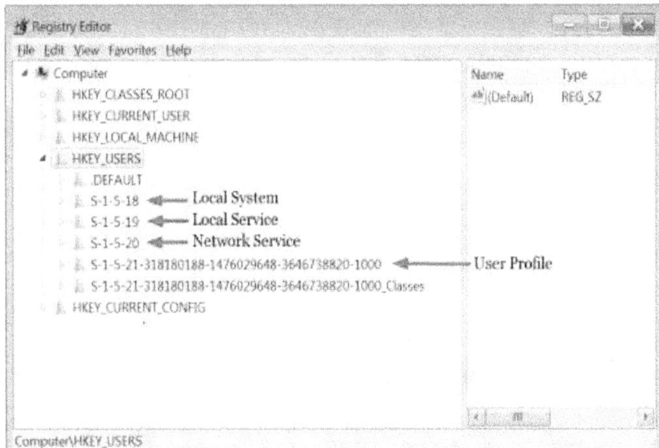

Security Identifiers (SID)

Under HKEY_USERS, you will see *Security Identifiers* (SID), which is part of Windows security. Windows uses a concept referred to as a *security principle*, which would include items such as computer accounts, user accounts, user groups, and other security-related objects.

On a local computer, the *Local Security Authority* (LSA) generates a SID for local security principles and then stores them in the local security database.

In Figure 4-3, you can see a SID of S-1-5-21-674973493-240844686-639060511-1002, which can be broken down into the following components:

[S]-[*version*]-[*identifier authority*]-[*domain identifier*]-[*relative identifier*]

The first 3 characters of a SID consist of:

S: A SID always begins with S

1: SID version

5: Identifier authority (5 is NT authority)

The following string of numbers (21-674973493-240844686-639060511) is the *domain identifier*.

The last 4 bytes of the SID is a *relative identifier* (RID), which is the account or group. Some of the common RIDs are:

500	Administrator
501	Guest
1000+	User Accounts

Microsoft lists well-known security identifiers on their website:

http://support.microsoft.com/kb/q243330

Operating System

Now that you have a good understanding of Windows time stamps and the registry, you can check the suspect's operating system. This is an important step before you begin your analysis, because you need to know what type of artifacts you are going to find and where they are located. Where are the user's documents or recent folder located? How is data being stored? If the suspect deleted something, can it be recovered? All of these questions and many others start to become easier to answer once you know what operating system the suspect was using.

The operating system information is stored in the SOFTWARE hive. This is located in:

```
C:\Windows\System32\config
```

Note: This current version of Autopsy (4.3) has issues opening the System32 folder since there is a large amount of data in it.

To view the time zone information stored in the SOFTWARE hive, you need to run another built-in module. Click Tools ▶ Run Ingest Modules ▶ Tucker.E01. When the Run Ingest Modules window opens, check Recent Activity and then click Start.

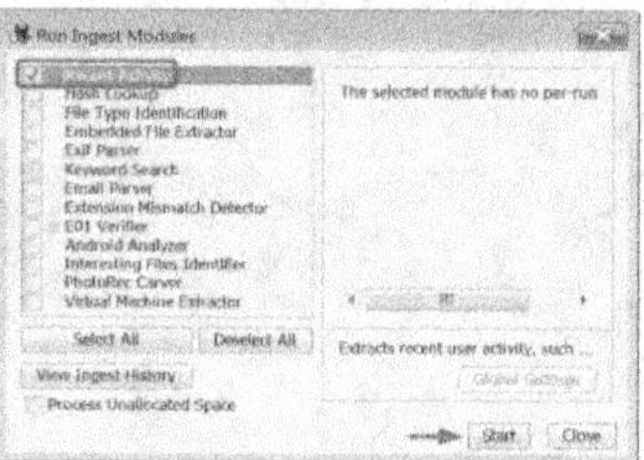

The Recent Activity module will pull web browser history data and important registry information so you do not have to manually find the data. However, it is still important to know where this information is being pulled from so you could manually find and verify the results if necessary. We will further cover where this data is stored in the registry as we view the results.

Once the Recent Activity module finishes running, you can click on Results ▶ Extracted Content ▶ Operating System Information. The last entry in the table pane shows that the operating system is Windows 8.1 Pro. It also shows that the owner of the computer is simply just Windows User (see ▆▆▆▆▆). This information has been extracted from the SOFTWARE hive and is stored under the following subkey:

```
Microsoft\Windows NT\Current Version
```

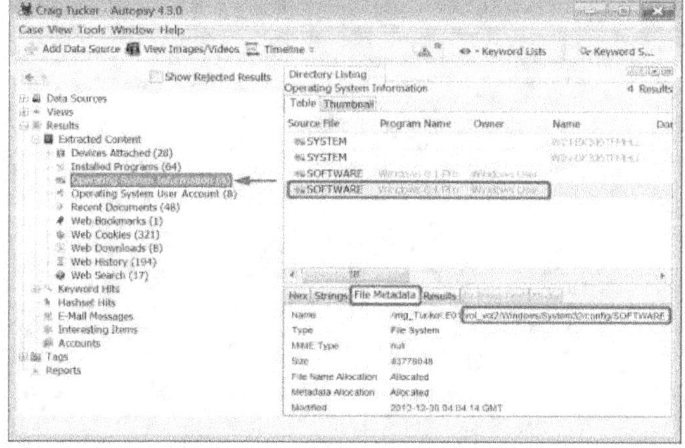

Note: There is another SOFTWARE entry in the table pane because there are backups for each registry hive.

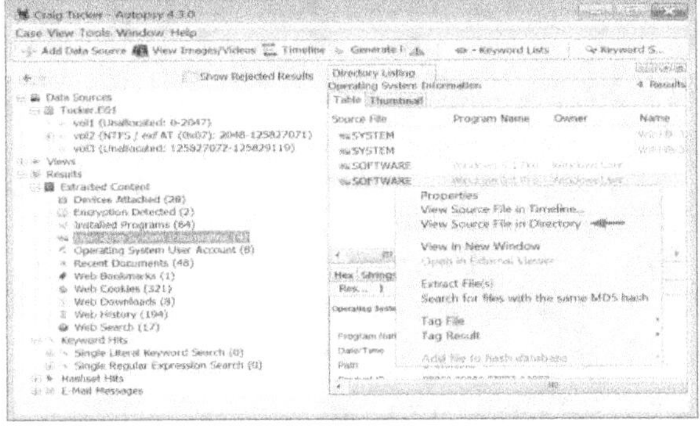

Registry Explorer

The information that Autopys extracts from the SYSTEM hive is useful, but it is very limited. If you want to further explore the user's registry and find more information, you will need to use another tool. For this case, we are going to use the tool called Registry Explorer. You can download it from:

https://ericzimmerman.github.io/

To use the tool, you will need to extract the registry hives from Autopsy. First, you need to right-click SOFTWARE in the table pane and select

This will take you to the config folder where the registry hives are stored. You will want to export out the SOFTWARE, SYSTEM, and SAM hive from the config folder.

To do this, click the first hive then press the Control key while clicking on the other hives. This will highlight all three files. Right-click one of the hives in the table pane and select Extract File(s).

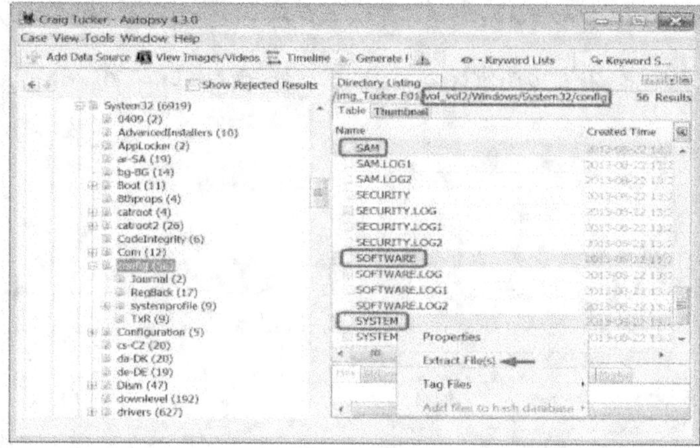

A Save window will open, and you need to create a folder to export the registry hives to. Once you have an export folder, click Save.

Note: Sometimes when Autopsy exports these registry hives, they attach a number to the name. Some tools may not recognize or open these renamed files. If Autopsy does attach a number to the SAM, SYSTEM, or SOFTWARE hive name in the export folder, you will need to navigate to your case export folder and then right-click on each hive and select Rename. Rename each one to their exact name without the numbers.

Once you have the registry hives exported, open the Registry Explorer tool and click File ► Load Offline Hive.

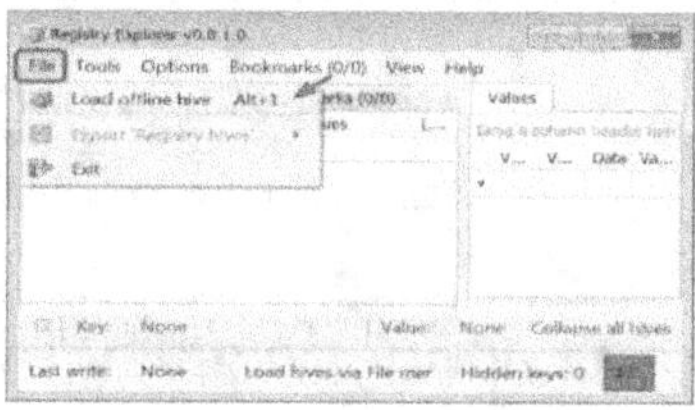

Navigate to where you exported the registry hives and select SOFTWARE hive to open. Once the tool opens the SOFTWARE hive, you need to go to the following subkey:

```
Microsoft\Windows NT\Current Version
```

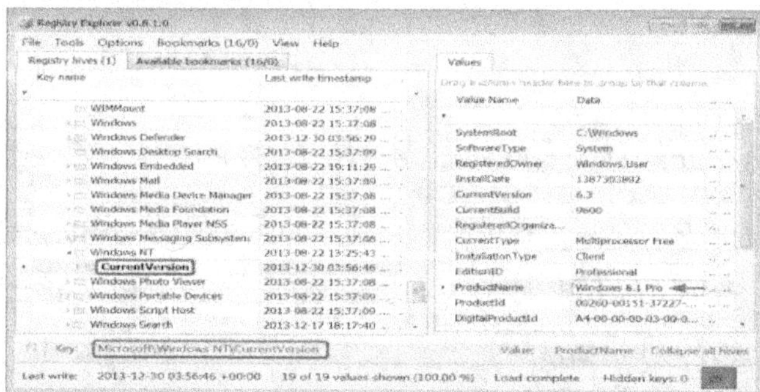

Time Zone

While Autopsy already pulled the operating system information with its module, there is some information in the registry that it does not pull. To find the time zone information in the registry, you will need to look at the SYSTEM hive. Open up the SYSTEM hive with Registry Explorer.

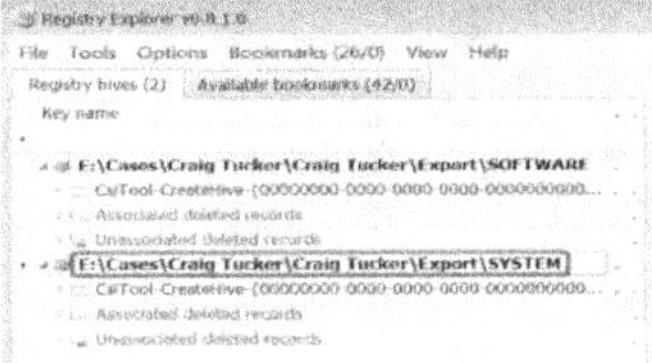

Note: When navigating through Registry Explorer and the subkeys, always look under the top key "CsiTool-CreateHive". From there, navigate to the subkey path you are directed to.

Once you have the SYSTEM hive opened, navigate to the following subkey:

```
[CurrentControlSet]\Control\TimeZoneInformation
```

You will notice a subkey called ControlSet001. In other images, you may see two or more subkeys with the name ControlSet, such as ControlSet002 and ControlSet003.

If there are multiple control sets in SYSTEM, then you need to know which one is current. You can navigate to the Select subkey and it will show you a value for the current control set. In this case, it is showing 1 as the current control set.

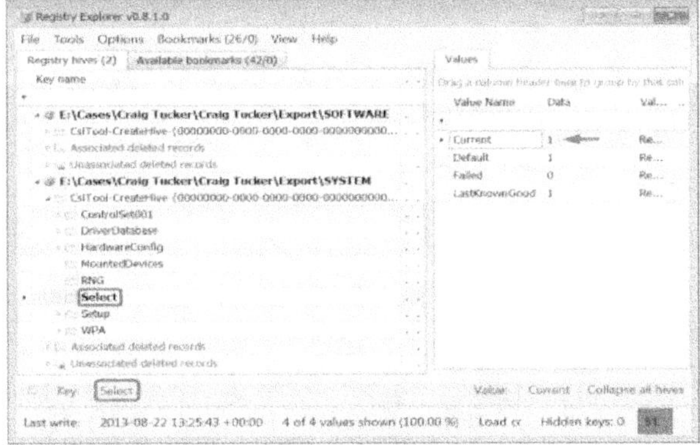

Now that you know the current control set, navigate to:

```
ControlSet001\Control\TimeZoneInformation
```

Under TimeZoneInformation there are two important values to look at. The first value is the TimeZoneKeyName, and Registry Explorer decodes the value data to plain text. The other value is ActiveTimeBias, and it shows how many minutes the system is off from UTC. For this computer, it's 480 minutes off from UTC. If you divide that by 60, you get 8 hours, which is the Pacific Standard Time Zone

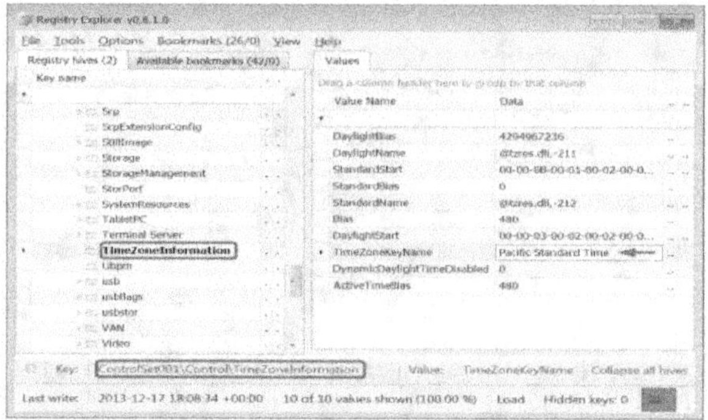

Identify Computer Users

The next section you will want to focus on when looking at registry data is identifying the computer users.

Understanding who was using the computer is a key part of your analysis. If your suspect was the only one that had access to the computer, then it makes it much easier to tie that person back to any activity on the computer. However, if other people were using it, you need to know who had access to what and which user account you need to focus on.

To view the user account information, select on Results ▶ Extracted Content ▶ Operating System User Account. There are several users listed, but if you remember from the User Profiles section, most of these are default accounts and default security identifiers (SIDs). In this case, there is only one user account, which is Craig. This user account has a SID of "S-1-5-21-1049150138-4017234595-3791460656-1001" and the RID is "1001".

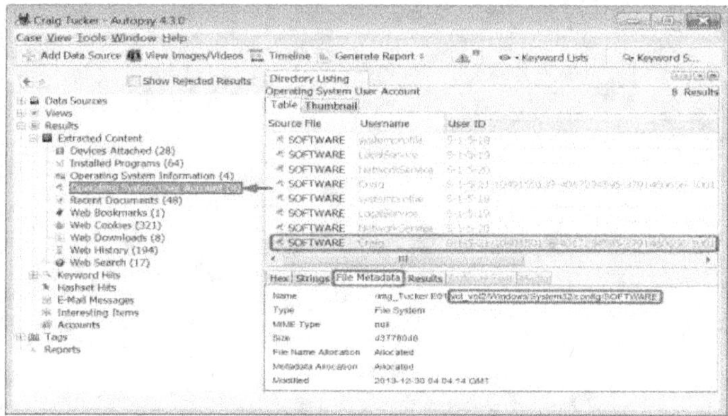

Note: There are duplicate entries for the user accounts because there are backups for each registry hive.

To find more information that Autopsy does not extract from the registry on users, look at the SOFTWARE hive in Registry Explorer. You need to navigate to the following subkey:

```
Microsoft\Windows NT\CurrentVersion\ProfileList
```

Under the ProfileList, there are four subkeys. The names of these four subkeys are the SIDs. The first three SIDs are defaults, and the last one is the user

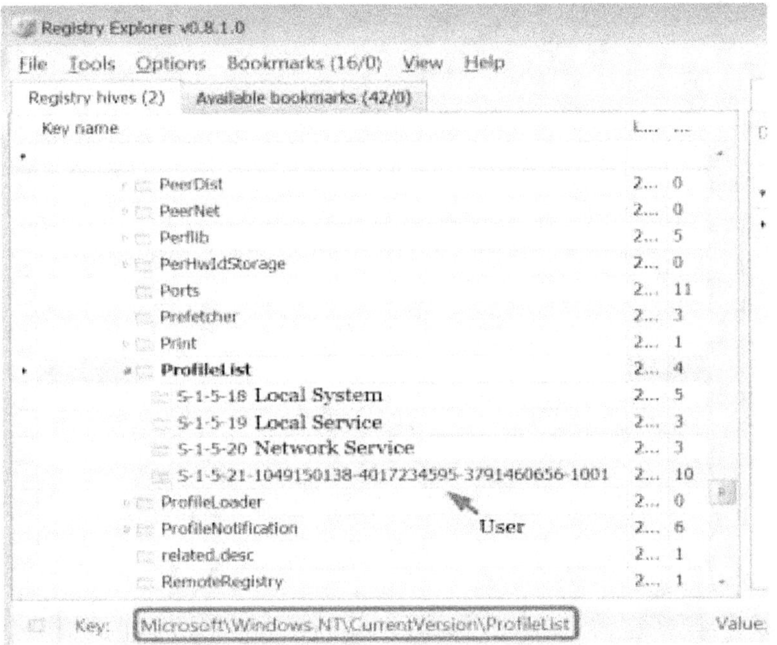

In this case, there is only one user account with a SID of "S-1-5-21-1049150138-4017234595-3791460656-1001" and the RID is "1001". You can easily identify this profile to the user account called Craig by looking at the ProfileImagePath value.

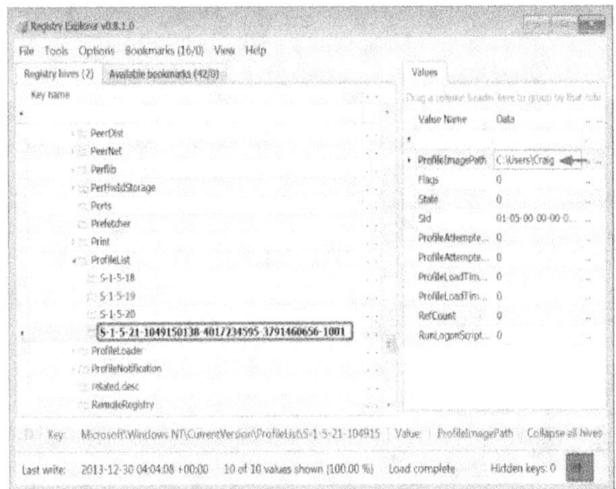

The next place you can look at user accounts is the SAM hive. This hive is the Security Account Manager (SAM). You already exported this hive from Autopsy, so go ahead and open the hive in Registry Explorer. Go to the following subkey of the SAM hive:

```
SAM\Domains\Account\Users
```

Under the Users subkey, there are 3 subkeys listed. These subkeys are the hex values of the user's relative identifier (RID). If you were to convert these hex values to decimal, they would decode as the following:

000001F4 = 500

000001F5 = 501

000003E9 = 1001

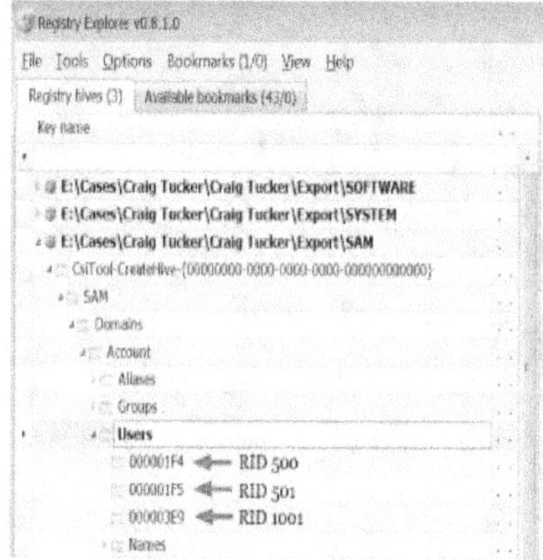

Since you already know that the actual user account, Craig, has a *RID* of 1001, select the 000003E9 subkey. This subkey stores a lot of information about the user account Craig. Information such as if the user account is disabled, how many times they logged in, and if the account has a password is mostly embedded within the values named F and V.

Login Password

When a user sets a login password in Windows, the password is not stored in clear text. A hash value of the password is stored within the SAM hive in the V value.

From a security standpoint, Microsoft did not just store a hash value of the user's password. As an added security measure to secure the NTLM hashes, the hash values are protected with Syskey. Syskey is basically an encryption key that is scattered throughout the SYSTEM hive, which is unique to a given system AND user.

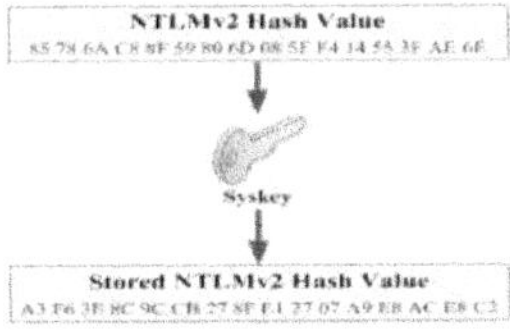

When a user types his password at the login prompt, the password is then hashed and compared against the stored hash in V. If the hash values match, then the user will successfully login to the operating system.

You can attempt to break the user's password by using a freeware tool called Ophcrack. This tool will also help determine which user accounts are password protected. The newest version of this tool (3.7) can be downloaded from:

```
http://ophcrack.sourceforge.net
```

To use Ophcrack and attempt to break the user's login password, you need to first export out the SAM and SYSTEM hives. Ophcrack uses the encrypted NTLMv2 hash value from the SAM hive and Syskey from the SYSTEM hive to reveal the actual NTLMv2 hash value. Once you have an actual hash value, Ophcrack will compare it to a rainbow table to find the password.

Note: A rainbow table is a pre-calculated dictionary full of hash values. Each hash value matches a password combination. Ophcrack uses the tables to compare the hash value stored in SAM, and tells you the password that matches the hash value.

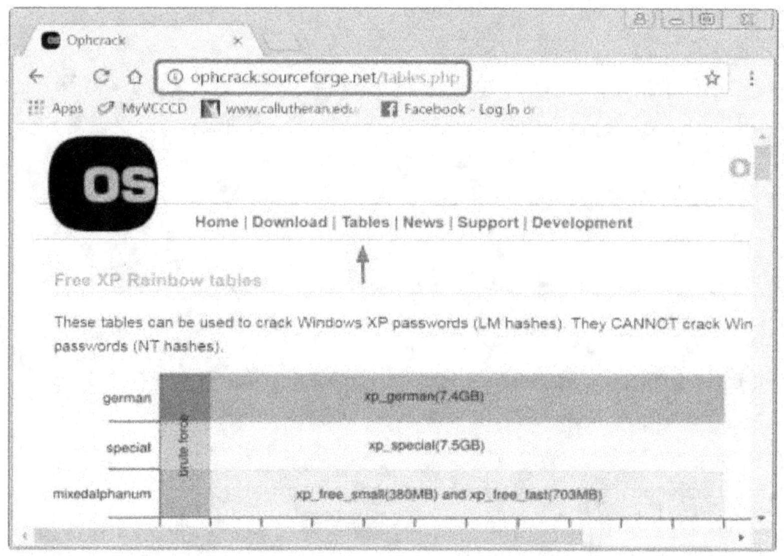

Open the Ophcrack tool and click Load ▶ Encrypted SAM.

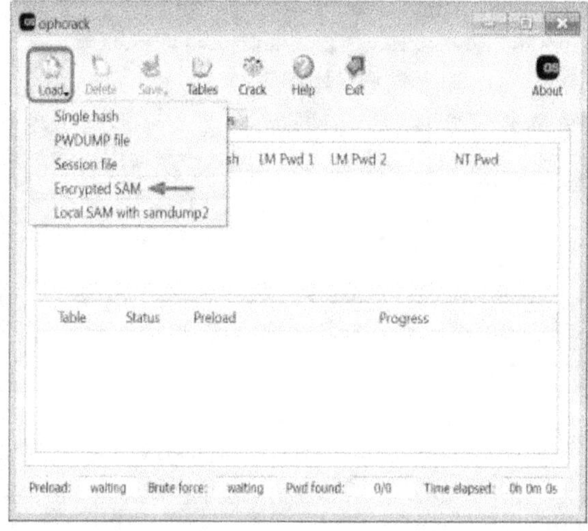

Ophcrack will open a window for you to navigate to your case export folder. Highlight the Export folder and click Select Folder

Note: Make sure you took out the numbers in the SYSTEM and SAM hive and renamed them to just SYSTEM and SAM. Ophcrack will not recognize the files if they have numbers in the name.

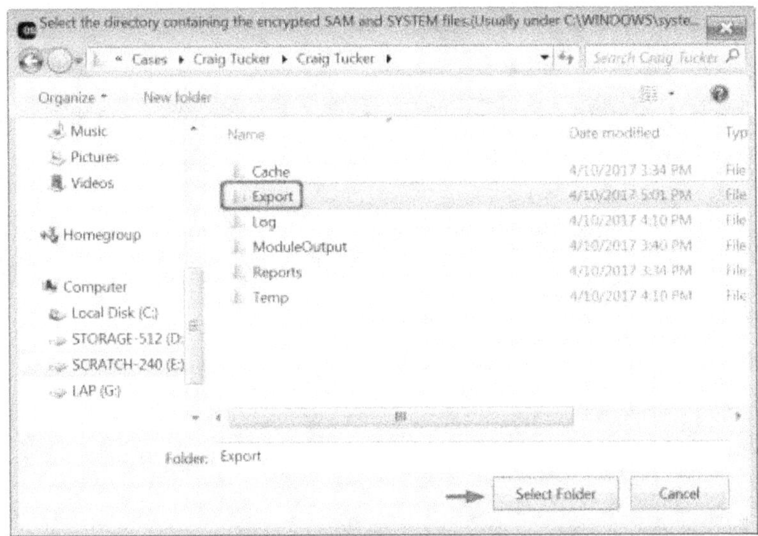

After it loads, Ophcrack will show three users. The first two are the disabled Administrator and Guest user accounts. The third user account is Craig, and his decrypted hash value is shown as "85786ac88f59806d085ff414553fae6e." Before you crack Craig's login password, you need to install the Vista Free rainbow table. Click Tables in the top bar of Ophcrack. A Table Selection window will open and you need to highlight the Vista Free and then click Install.

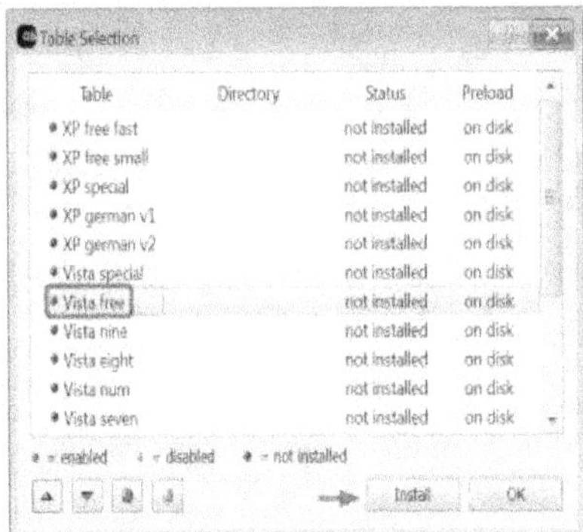

After clicking Install, navigate to where you downloaded the Vista free table from Ophcrack. You want to then click

Select folder on the folder that you extracted from the downloaded zip from Ophcrack

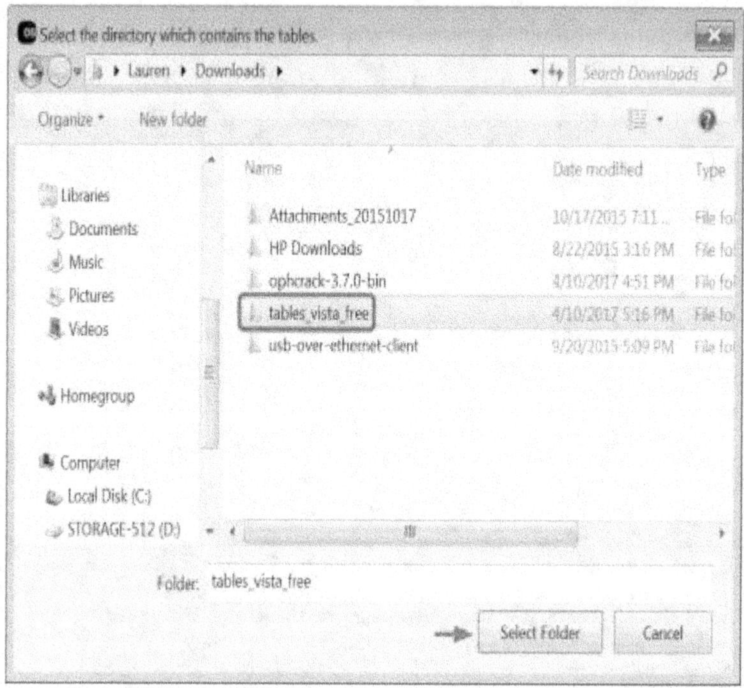

On the Table Selection window in Ophcrack, click OK. On the main Ophcrack window, you should see Vista free under Tables now. Click the Crack button in the top bar to crack Craig's login password.

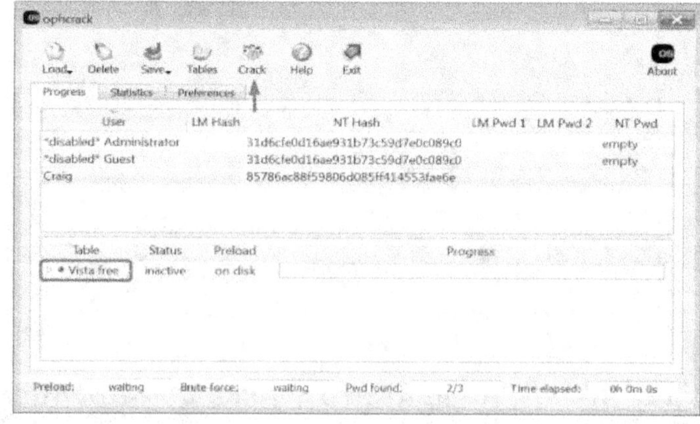

If Ophcrack successfully finds a match, it will report back that hash value's matching password. In this case, Craig's password is hungry123. Knowing this password may help you break other passwordprotected files.

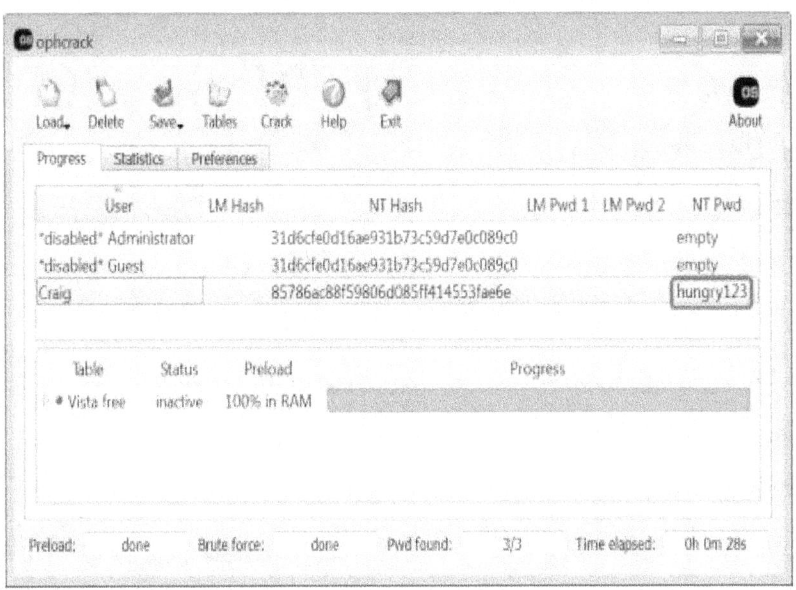

Note: Craig's login password "hungry123" is a very simple password and that is why you are able to break it with a smaller rainbow table. If the password had upper case letters, symbols, and was longer, you would need a much larger rainbow table to break the password, and it would take much more time to crack.

Chapter VII:
Computer (Digital) Forensic Tools & Software

Digital forensic is a process of preservation, identification, extraction, and documentation of computer evidence which can be used by the court of law. There are many tools that help you to make this process simple and easy. These applications provide complete reports that can be used for legal procedures.

Following is a handpicked list of Digital Forensic Toolkits, with their popular features and website links. The list contains both open source(free) and commercial(paid) software.

1) ProDiscover Forensic

prodiscover®
COMPUTER FORENSICS

ProDiscover Forensic is a computer security app that allows you to locate all the data on a computer disk. It can protect evidence and create quality reports for the use of legal procedures. This tool allows you to extract EXIF(Exchangeable Image File Format) information from JPEG files.

Features:

- This product supports Windows, Mac, and Linux file systems.

- You can preview and search for suspicious files quickly.
- This Digital forensics software creates a copy of the entire suspected disk to keep the original evidence safe.
- This tool helps you to see internet history.
- You can import or export .dd format images.
- It enables you to add comments to evidence of your interest.
- ProDiscover Forensic supports VMware to run a captured image.

Link: https://www.prodiscover.com

2) Sleuth Kit (+Autopsy)

Sleuth Kit (+Autopsy) is a Windows based utility tool that makes forensic analysis of computer systems easier. This tool allows you to examine your hard drive and smartphone.

Features:

- You can identify activity using a graphical interface effectively.

- This application provides analysis for emails.
- You can group files by their type to find all documents or images.
- It displays a thumbnail of images to quick view pictures.
- You can tag files with the arbitrary tag names.
- The Sleuth Kit enables you to extract data from call logs, SMS, contacts, etc.
- It helps you to flag files and folders based on path and name.

Link: https://www.sleuthkit.org

CAINE is a Ubuntu-based app that offers a complete forensic environment that provides a graphical interface. This tool can be integrated into existing software tools as a module. It automatically extracts a timeline from RAM.

Features:

- It supports the digital investigator during the four phases of the digital investigation.
- It offers a user-friendly interface.
- You can customize features of CAINE.

3) CAINE

- This software offers numerous user-friendly tools.

Link: https://www.caine-live.net

---

4) PDF to Excel Convertor

Acrobat PDF to Excel Convertor transfers PDF data and content right into an Excel spreadsheet. This converted file proves helpful for tracking down cybercriminals from anywhere in the world. This computer forensic tool supports both partial and batch conversion.

Features:

- Allows you to work from anywhere
- Super-fast with high-quality output
- Allows you to work from anywhere

- It retains the original layout and formatting

---

5) Google Takeout Convertor

Google Takeout Convertor converts archived email messages from Google Takeout along with all attachments. This software helps investigate officers to extract, process, and interpret the factual evidence.

Features:

- Batch multiple export files from the Google Takeout account at once to save time and effort.

- This computer forensic app also offers a batch mode feature that helps you save time and effort.
- Supports converting Google Takeout files to the most popular cloud-based email service.
- Offers dual-mode function for loading and converting Google Takeout files/folders.
- Supported platform: Windows

---

6) PALADIN

PALADIN is Ubuntu based tool that enables you to simplify a range of forensic tasks. This Digital forensics software provides more than 100 useful tools for investigating any malicious material. This tool helps you to simplify your forensic task quickly and effectively.

Features:

- It provides both 64-bit and 32-bit versions.
- This tool is available on a USB thumb drive.
- This toolbox has open-source tools that help you to search for the required information effortlessly.
- This tool has more than 33 categories that assist you in

accomplishing a
cyber forensic task.
Link: https://sumuri.com/
software/paladin/

---

7) EnCase

Encase is an application
that helps you to recover
evidence from hard drives.
It allows you to conduct
an in-depth analysis of
files to collect proof like
documents, pictures, etc.
Features:

- You can acquire
  data from numerous
  devices, including
  mobile phones,
  tablets, etc.
- It is one of the best
  mobile forensic tools
  that enables you to
  produce complete
  reports for

maintaining
evidence integrity.

- You can quickly
  search, identify, as
  well as prioritize
  evidence.
- Encase-forensic
  helps you to unlock
  encrypted evidence.
- It is one of the best
  digital forensics
  tools that automates
  the preparation of
  evidence.
- You can perform
  deep and triage
  (severity and
  priority of defects)
  analysis.

Link: https://www.guidan
cesoftware.com/encase-
forensic

---

8) SIFT Workstation

SIFT Workstation is a computer forensics distribution based on Ubuntu. It is one of the best computer forensic tools that provides a digital forensic and incident response examination facility.
Features:

- It can work on a 64-bit operating system.
- This tool helps users to utilize memory in a better way.
- It automatically updates the DFIR (Digital Forensics and Incident Response) package.
- You can install it via SIFT-CLI (Command-Line Interface) installer.

- This tool contains numerous latest forensic tools and techniques.

Link: https://www.sans.org/tools/sift-workstation/

---

9) FTK Imager

FTK Imager is a forensic toolkit i developed by AccessData that can be used to get evidence. It can create copies of data without making changes to the original evidence. This tool allows you to specify criteria, like file size, pixel size, and data type, to reduce the amount of irrelevant data.
Features:

- It provides a wizard-driven

approach to detect cybercrime.

- This program offers better visualization of data using a chart.
- You can recover passwords from more than 100 applications.
- It has an advanced and automated data analysis facility.
- FTK Imager helps you to manage reusable profiles for different investigation requirements.
- It supports pre and post-processing refinement.

Link: https://accessdata.com/products-services/forensic-toolkit-ftk

10) Magnet RAM capture

Magnet RAM capture records the memory of a suspected computer. It allows investigators to recover and analyze valuable items which are found in memory.

Features:

- You can run this app while minimizing overwritten data in memory.
- It enables you to export captured memory data and upload it into analysis tools like magnet AXIOM and magnet IEF.
- This app supports a vast range of

Windows operating systems.

- Magnet RAM capture supports RAM acquisition.

Link: https://www.magnetforensics.com/resources/magnet-ram-capture/

---

11) X-Ways Forensics

X-Ways

X-Ways is software that provides a work environment for computer forensic examiners. This program is supports disk cloning and imaging. It enables you to collaborate with other people who have this tool.

Features:

- It has ability to read partitioning and file system structures inside .dd image files.
- You can access disks, RAIDs (Redundant array of independent disk), and more.
- It automatically identifies lost or deleted partitions.
- This tool can easily detect NTFS (New Technology File System) and ADS (Alternate Data Streams).
- X-Ways Forensics supports bookmarks or annotations.
- It has the ability to analyze remote computers.
- You can view and edit binary data by using templates.
- It provides write protection for

maintaining data authenticity.

Link: http://www.x-ways.net/forensics/

---

12) Wireshark

Wireshark is a tool that analyzes a network packet. It can be used to for network testing and troubleshooting. This tool helps you to check different traffic going through your computer system.

Features:

- It provides rich VoIP (Voice over Internet Protocol) analysis.
- Capture files compressed with gzip can be decompressed easily.
- Output can be exported to XML (Extensible Markup Language), CSV (Comma Separated Values) file, or plain text.
- Live data can be read from the network, blue-tooth, ATM, USB, etc.
- Decryption support for numerous protocols that include IPsec (Internet Protocol Security), SSL (Secure Sockets Layer), and WEP (Wired Equivalent Privacy).
- You can apply intuitive analysis, coloring rules to the packet.
- Allows you to read or write file in any format.

Link: https://www.wiresh
ark.org

---

13) Registry Recon

Registry Recon is a computer forensics tool used to extract, recover, and analyze registry data from Windows OS. This program can be used to efficiently determine external devices that have been connected to any PC.
Features:

- It supports Windows XP, Vista, 7, 8, 10, and other operating systems.
- This tool automatically recovers valuable NTFS data.
- You can integrate it with the Microsoft Disk Manager utility tool.
- Quickly mount all VSCs (Volume Shadow Copies) VSCs within a disk.
- This program rebuilds the active registry database.

Link: https://arsenalrecon
.com/products/

---

14) Volatility Framework

Volatility Framework is software for memory analysis and forensics. It is one of the best Forensic imaging tools that helps you to test the runtime state of a system using the data found in RAM. This app allows you to collaborate with your teammates.
Features:

- It has API that allows you to lookups of PTE (Page Table Entry) flags quickly.
- Volatility Framework supports KASLR (Kernel Address Space Layout Randomization).
- This tool provides numerous plugins for checking Mac file operation.
- It automatically runs Failure command when a service fails to start multiple times.

Link: https://www.volatili tyfoundation.org

---

15) Xplico

Xplico is an open-source forensic analysis app. It supports HTTP(Hypertext Transfer Protocol), IMAP (Internet Message Access Protocol), and more. Features:

- You can get your output data in the SQLite database or MySQL database.
- This tool gives you real time collaboration.
- No size limit on data entry or the number of files.
- You can easily create any kind of dispatcher to organize the extracted data in a useful way.
- It is one of the best open source forensic tools that support both IPv4 and IPv6.

- You can perform reserve DNS lookup from DNS packages having input files.
- Xplico provides PIPI (Port Independent Protocol Identification) feature to support digital forensic.

Link: https://www.xplico.org

---

16) e-fense
E-fense is a tool that helps you to meet your computer forensics and cybersecurity needs. It allows you to discover files from any device in one simple to use interface.
Features:

- It gives protection from malicious behavior, hacking, and policy violations.
- You can acquire internet history, memory, and screen capture from a system onto a USB thumb drive.
- This tool has a simple to use interface that enables you to achieve your investigation goal.
- E-fense supports multithreading, that means you can execute more than one thread simultaneously.

Link: http://www.e-fense.com/products.php

---

17) Crowdstrike
Crowdstrike is digital forensic software that provides threat

intelligence, endpoint security, etc. It can quickly detect and recover from cybersecurity incidents. You can use this tool to find and block attackers in real time. Features:

- It is one of the best cyber forensics tools that help you to manage system vulnerabilities.
- It can automatically analyze malware.
- You can secure your virtual, physical, and cloud-based data center.